Cats

Rec... ...bout
...Purchase, Care,
and Nutrition

Brigitte Eilert-Overbeck

Contents

4 The World of Cats

5 Living with a Cat
6 A Brief Cultural History of Cats
8 Cat Portraits
12 Of Cats and Kittens
13 **Expert Tip:** Key Phases of Development
14 **At a Glance:** The Graceful Hunter
16 Am I a Cat Person?
18 A New Family Member

20 Your Feline Companion

21 Fostering a Good Partnership
22 Decisions, Decisions...
23 **Expert Tip:** How to Recognize a Healthy Cat
24 Everything a Cat Needs: Essential Equipment

26 A Warm Welcome: Helping Your Cat Adjust
28 The Indoor Cat and Her Territory
30 **Etiquette for Cats**
31 At Home with Other Animals

32 Health and Happiness

33 Keeping Your Cat in Top Form
34 *Bon Appétit!* The Correct Cat Diet
37 Grooming and Hygiene
39 Prevention and Treatment
40 **Expert Tip:** Caution—Poisonous Hazards
41 A Quick Recovery, the Easy Way
42 Feline First-Aid Kit
43 Homeopathic Medicine

44 Understanding Your Cat

45 Nurturing a Good Relationship
46 Cat Communication
47 **Expert Tip:** How Cats Learn to Recognize Their Names
48 How Cats Express Their Moods
50 The "Arrangement": Training Your Cat
52 Safely Roaming Outdoors
54 Playtime for You and Your Pet
58 Dealing with Changes
59 **Expert Tip:** Saying Good-bye

Extras

60 Index
62 Information
64 SOS – What to Do?

The World of Cats

Many thousands of years ago, the African wildcat relocated her hunting grounds to human settlements. This was the beginning of an infinite love story, and today, domestic cats are found the world over. After all, cats and humans are very well suited for each other!

Living with a Cat

For thousands of years cats have been part of our world, and they have thoroughly established themselves in our hearts. In U.S. households alone there are almost 88.3 million purring felines. Domestic cats are attached to their homes more than any other animal. Beyond that, they are dedicated to their owners, more than they are to other cats. They see their owners as "super cats," the companions with whom they do not need to compete—not for territory, not for prey, not for a mate. People provide warmth and attention, and spoil their cats by stroking them and enticing them to play. Indeed, humans have essentially taken over the role of mother cat. In the world of humans, cats are allowed to remain children, and they are more than happy to do that. Yet cats also belong to another world, the world they have inherited from their wild ancestors. In that world, they are still highly developed predators—fast and skilled hunters with keen senses and lithe bodies. Nature has equipped domestic cats with weapons that are just as effective as those of tigers, pumas, and leopards, except on a smaller scale. Apart from lions and cheetahs, all cat species are solitary hunters. Therefore, they do not have a hierarchical pack structure; no natural system of subordination and obedience. In her territory, the cat is her own boss.

Rules of the Game

Orders, even when given by the "super cat," have no meaning for felines; they are studiously ignored. However, our domesticated cats have inherited from their wild ancestors the readiness to come to an "arrangement" with other cats and to accept certain rules. Once you understand this, there are no obstacles in the path toward a pleasant communal life with your cat.

A Brief Cultural History of Cats

Cats are different from all other animals that have been domesticated over the course of human history. In contrast to dogs, cattle, sheep, and pigs, cats—in their external appearance—have changed very little from their wild ancestors. Similarly, they have not surrendered their hunting skills: A cat cannot resist chasing mice and, if need be, will "hunt" for toys. And yet, domestic cats are also distinctly different from their ancestors. They relate far more to humans and largely depend on us to survive.

Born Hunters

Cats were still wild when humans had already domesticated other animals. Cats came to man on their own impulse, drawn by the hordes of mice that flocked to the food humans had begun to store. Cats, like man, profited from mutual territorial use: One captured easy prey and the other had his harvest saved from the rodents. These unequal partners took a liking to each other. Moreover, they had similar preferences: for a protective roof over

Rough terrain? Not for a cat! Equipped with well-padded paws and a fantastic sense of balance, she walks on tiptoes and with total surefootedness along the top of a picket fence.

their heads, for the reliability of a daily routine, for certain comforts, and—as ancient depictions of cats show—for friendly, tender contact.

Ancestral Mother: The African Wildcat

The ancestral mother of all domestic (house) cats is the African wildcat (*Felis silvestris lybica*). It inhabits vast areas of Africa as well as the northern part of the Arabian Peninsula. As shown recently by the geneticist Carlos Driscoll, the ancestors of all house cats throughout the world originally came from that particular region of the Middle East.

Gods and Demons

In ancient Egypt, the tame descendants of the African wildcat even assumed the role of gods. The sun god, Ra—who took the shape of a cat—attacked the Snake of Darkness; the cat-headed moon goddess, Bastet, was responsible for love, fertility, happiness, and wealth. Cats were also sacred to the Egyptian mother goddess, Isis. In ancient Roman mythology, cats accompanied Diana, goddess of the moon and the hunt, and they were at home in Asian temples and palaces. In Christendom they were considered to be the favorite animals of the Virgin Mary—until the outbreak of witch-hunting mania in the late Middle Ages. For centuries, cats were persecuted, tortured, killed, and nearly exterminated. Only in the early eighteenth century were they reinstated as pets.

Shipping Out

The domestication of cats was completed about 3,500 years ago. With that, they gradually found their way from the Middle East to the rest of the world. Export prohibitions issued by the ancient Egyptians did not prevent these velvety-pawed

Isn't there something rustling in the tall grass? When stalking prey, the concentrating hunter does not miss the slightest movement or the softest sound.

animals from getting onto trading ships. It was not long before the proverbial ship's cat became commonplace, used principally for protecting the freight against rats and mice. This led to the worldwide distribution of cats, who readily adapted to new environments. The first longhaired cats appeared in the mountainous regions of Asia Minor, the ancestors of the modern Persian and semi-longhaired cats. Very slender cats with short hair, the ancestors of Siamese and Burmese cats, developed in Southeast Asia. Cats with a compact body and denser fur (with an insulating undercoat) developed in temperate climatic regions, the ancestors of today's house cat. This type of cat is now bred as the European Shorthair. Similarly, the "forest cat" breeds, such as the Maine Coon, the Norwegian Forest Cat, and the Siberian, developed their thick coats in adaptation to climate.

Calm and well-balanced

Persian

Origin Persian cats were first bred in England.
The breed was developed by crossing angora cats
(the former name for all longhaired cats) with
shorthaired cats.

Appearance With their majestic coats, Persian
cats are deserving successors to the elegant longhaired cats that lived principally at royal courts.
They have the longest fur of all breeds: a silky, flow-
ing fur with an almost mane-like neck collar. The
body is strong and slightly compact, the legs are
short and stout, and the head is broad with a characteristic snub nose and large, shiny eyes.

Character The Persian is calm, but not spiritless;
easy-going and even-tempered, but not lazy; affectionate, but not insistent. She can easily be kept in
an apartment and needs plenty of loving attention
from her owner—including the essential daily
grooming of her long fur.

Robust and uncomplicated

Maine Coon

Origin The Maine Coon, with her raccoon-like tail,
was first spotted in the northeastern United States,
in the state of Maine. She is one of the so-called
forest cat breeds, which did not originate through
selective breeding but instead developed totally on
their own. Among her ancestors are longhaired cats
that were brought ashore by sailors.

Appearance Maine Coons are true outdoor cats
and real heavyweights: Males can reach a weight of
up to 20 pounds (9 kilograms). Their coat's semi-
long guard hairs repel water, and a very dense
undercoat keeps them nice and warm during the
winter. The Maine Coon has an angular snout, large
eyes, and large ears with attractive tufts of fur.

Character This cat has an uncomplicated, friendly
nature, remaining calm even amid the chaos of
family activities, and gets along well with other animals. She likes to be outside and hunts for mice
with great enthusiasm.

Uncomplicated and leisurely
British Shorthair

Origin As its name indicates, this breed originated in Great Britain. Its ancestors were domesticated cats and Persian cats. The British Shorthair has been bred in its current form since the 1950s.

Appearance The British Shorthair is roundish, compact, and stout. Her head is broad with full cheeks, small ears, and large, round eyes that have an orange- to copper-colored glow. She has very dense fur and a thick, medium-long tail. British Shorthairs are bred in many colors; the "blue" variety looks very similar to the Chartreux breed and is often erroneously referred to as a Chartreux.

Character British Shorthair cats are as robust, friendly, and good natured as they look, and they "talk" with their owners in a pleasant, soft voice. They can be kept indoors without problems, and they get along well with other cats and animals. Because of their easy-going character, they fit in readily with active family life.

Intelligent and curious
Bengal

Origin This breed developed in the United States around 1960, from crosses with wild Bengal cats (*Felis bengalensis*, also known as Asian Leopard Cats) with domesticated cats and pedigree cats, respectively. It is sometimes referred to as "Leopardette."

Appearance The Bengal cat is large, slender, and muscular. Her dense, fine shorthair coat is covered with brown to black patches, spots, and rosettes. Thus attired, the cat actually looks like a miniature version of a leopard. With her long legs, the Bengal is an excellent climber and jumper.

Character Bengal cats are friendly to other cats and get along well with other animals. Moreover, they are very curious and extremely intelligent. These mini-leopards like to take charge of their owners; they are very clever in play, as well as quite quick to learn. Some of them enjoy splashing around in water to such an extent that they can even be taken into the shower.

---

needs frequent grooming   ideal for outdoor living   ideal for indoor living   needs lots of exercise

Intelligent and elegant
Abyssinian

Origin Originally from Africa, the Abyssinian was being bred in England as early as the end of the nineteenth century. The breed has been recognized worldwide since the late 1940s.

Appearance Everything about this cat is elegant: the long legs, the lithe, medium-sized body, the slightly wedge-shaped head with large ears and almond-shaped eyes, the long, pointed tail, and, certainly not the least, the short, dense, silky coat. The individual hairs are subdivided into light and dark bands, creating the Abyssinian's signature "ticked" coat and enhancing its wildcat appeal.

Character Abyssinians are very intelligent, alert, and temperamental, and sometimes also some-what jumpy. They are excellent hunters and need a lot of stimulation, activity, and movement. Friendly and devoted, they like to have their owners around at all times.

Devoted and slightly shy
Russian Blue

Origin Sailors from the Russian Arctic seaport of Arkhangelsk brought this cat to Western Europe for the first time in 1860. Russian Blues nearly became extinct in 1945, so many breeders crossed them with Siamese cats to maintain the breed.

Appearance Her slender but very athletic physique, together with her glowing green eyes and characteristic whiskers, make the Russian Blue a pleasure to behold. The dense, blue-gray coat with silvery sheen is not the least of her charms. The undercoat, which is the same length as the topcoat, and the guard hairs give the fur its plush texture; the sheen is produced by the transparent tips of the individual hairs.

Character Russian Blues are very well behaved and agreeable. They are attached to their trusted owners and reward them with devoted affection. However, toward strangers they are likely to be more reserved. They are intimidated by loud noise. These cats are suitable for small apartments.

Sociable and self-assured
Siberian

Origin Siberian cats originally came from Russia
and the Ukraine. Just like the Maine Coon and
the Norwegian Forest Cat, this breed developed
naturally.

Appearance The Siberian cat is strong, muscular,
and of medium size. The wedge-shaped head is
nicely rounded and the almond-shaped eyes are
set far apart. The semi-long fur consists of smooth,
strong, water-repellent guard hairs and a dense,
soft undercoat to protect against the cold. In other
words, Siberians have a coat that is typical of forest
cats, with a conspicuous chest patch, "pants" on
the hind legs, and a magnificent tail. There are tufts
of fur between the toes and on the ears.

Character Siberians enjoy company; they like to
cuddle and play, but occasionally require an opportunity to withdraw. They are sufficiently self-
assured to indicate to their owners when they
prefer to be left alone.

Playful and cuddly
Birman

Origin If the legends are true, the "Sacred Birman"
is a temple cat from Southeast Asia. However, this
breed probably developed in southern France
from crosses between Siamese and longhaired
cats. It has been bred intensively since the middle
of the 1920s.

Appearance The Birman is strong and muscular,
with stout legs and light-colored, silky, semi-long to
long fur with little undercoat. Just like the Siamese,
this cat has shiny blue eyes and dark markings on
her face, ears, legs, and tail. Her paws are snow
white. The kittens are born with short, white fur.

Character Birman cats have a friendly nature and
get along well with other cats and animals. They
like to cuddle and play, and are very patient when
interacting with children. They are far more active
than Persians but significantly quieter than their
Siamese ancestors.

---

 needs frequent grooming   ideal for outdoor living   🏠 ideal for indoor living   ▤ needs lots of exercise

Of Cats and Kittens

Female cats (queens) are seasonally polyestrous, which means they go into heat—or become ready to mate—several times a year. If kept solely in artificial light, they may go into heat more frequently. The cat will roll on the ground, loudly vocalizing for a male (tomcat), and thus attracts the male cat population from the entire neighborhood. Before the actual breeding takes place, loud fights break out among the gathered toms. If the breeding is successful, kittens will follow in about nine weeks. A queen can give birth to from anywhere between one and eight kittens, the average being two to five.

Maternal Duties

Prior to giving birth, the pregnant female will look for a suitable location, where she will—within a few hours—deliver the kittens. With their first sips of mother's milk (colostrum), the young will also take in important immune substances, which protect the kittens for approximately two months against many infectious diseases. During the first four weeks of their lives, their mother cares for them virtually around the clock. She keeps them warm, monitors them, and nurses them. She also massages their tummies with her tongue and keeps the nest clean by removing their waste products.

New Beginnings

Kittens are born as little furballs with thin legs, weighing barely 4 ounces (100 grams). Blind, nearly deaf, and unable to maintain their body temperature, they are totally dependent on their mother. Yet they quickly make dramatic progress. At two weeks, they are already able to purr, perceive sounds, retract their claws, and recognize shapes with their baby-blue eyes. Six-week-old kittens already have complete hearing faculties, vastly improved vision, and all their milk teeth. They clean themselves just like adults, use the litter box, climb around, and play tag. If given the opportunity, they will even capture prey. The queen nurses them less and less frequently, and at the age of eight weeks, they are usually fully weaned.

Ready for human contact: Favorable experiences with people will become deeply imprinted in four- to seven-week-old kittens.

From Furball to Personality

The fluffy little furballs will turn into small personalities in virtually no time, each slightly different in character and temperament from the other siblings. However, the family bond remains important throughout their development. Kittens practice the behavior of adults when playing with each other and when around their mother. This is how they learn to get along with other cats. After 12 weeks (16 weeks at the latest) the kittens have learned their feline lessons, and can then conquer their human family and the new territory that comes with it. They are full of adventurous spirit; they are agile like acrobats, and their vision is as sharp as that of a lynx. Their milk teeth are replaced with permanent teeth after six months. The kittens will then become quieter, and at an age of seven to nine months, the wild times will be over and their sex drives will begin to awaken.

The Puberty Problem

You can tell male cats (toms) by their urine. Suddenly it will have an "aromatic fragrance" reminiscent of the cat house at the local zoo, and he will liberally spray it around as a potent advertisement for female cats in heat. While in heat, cats have only one thing on their minds, and the result is far too many kittens and not enough loving homes for them. The best solution for unplanned mating and pregnancy is to have your cat spayed or neutered. This procedure will not harm your cat, nor will it impair her further development. It takes at least one year for a cat to be fully mature. Many reach their ultimate size only after two years, and some toms reach maturity only after three years. Happily purring on the lap of her owner, even a full-grown cat feels like a well-protected kitten.

Key **Phases** of **Development**

TIPS FROM
CAT EXPERT
Brigitte Eilert-Overbeck

There are several imprinting (distinct learning) phases in the life of a kitten. During these phases, the course is set for the further development of the animal.

FROM THE SECOND WEEK onward, one of the most important phases begins, lasting until the end of the seventh week. Each positive experience your kitten has with the world during this time gives her a dose of confidence, as well as a sense of self-reliance. Gently introducing your kitten to family members and other people, and establishing a normal household routine, will help ensure that she grows up to be an open-minded cat.

FROM THE FOURTH TO THE SEVENTH WEEK kittens excel at establishing social contacts, especially with people. Stroking, cuddling, and playing are now very much desired. But don't forget the mother cat; she needs a cuddle, too!

FROM THE EIGHTH TO THE TWELVTH WEEK, kittens are distinctly "talkative." Try communicating with your kitten in a mixed cat/human dialect, which will prepare her for contact with her new human family.

The Graceful Hunter

Coat

A well-groomed cat's coat protects against minor injuries, UV radiation, and rain, and it is an excellent "air conditioner." It is also a means of expression: Angry or frightened cats raise their fur to make themselves look larger and intimidate the opponent.

Tail

The many muscles of the tail are key to maintaining balance. Cats use their tails as a rudder when jumping and as a balancing pole. The tail is also a mood barometer and a means of expression.

Paws

Cats walk on their tiptoes. This makes them ideal sprinters and jumpers, able to change direction even when running at top speed. The claws are versatile tools: They are used in climbing, fighting, or holding on to prey. Regular scratching is essential to keep the claws sharp.

Ears

Cat ears can hear more than human ears, even sounds within the high-frequency range. The outer ear helps the cat determine the direction of a particular sound. She can rotate these "sound funnels" nearly 180° to detect even very soft noises. Movements of the ears are also a good barometer for your cat's mood.

Eyes

A cat's vision is three-dimensional, and feline eyes are also very good at estimating distances. The eye's reflective coating amplifies light when it hits the retina, enlarging the pupil. Therefore, cats can see particularly well in the dark.

Nose

The nose is important for examining food, when encountering other cats, and during courtship. The tip of the nose (rhinarium) is also used for checking the temperature of an item before actually touching it.

Tongue

The cat's tongue, covered with tiny, thorny hooks, serves as a multipurpose tool. It is used as a washcloth and fur comb, as a scoop spoon for drinking, and as a rasp to remove meat remnants from the bones of prey.

Whiskers

The stiff and very sensitive hairs around the mouth, above the eyes, and on the backs of the front paws are the cat's antennae. She uses them to detect obstacles before actually touching them, and so is able to find her way in the dark. The whiskers are also used as feelers to sense prey and other foreign objects.

Am I a Cat Person?

There are approximately 88.3 million cats in U.S. households. There are more than 125 million cars traveling U.S. roadways, not including buses, trucks, and other large vehicles. At a first glance, these facts seem to have little to do with each other, but they underline how much the world has changed for our little feline hunter. Nowadays, where can a cat find a sufficient hunting ground? Where can she roam around without being in danger? More than ever before, our cats depend on our protection and care, as well as on our understanding of their complex nature.

What Your Cat Needs From You

Loyalty Cats can reach an age of about 20 years; some live even longer. If you are considering cat ownership, you must be willing to take on a long-term obligation. This means that you are prepared to take care of your cat in case of illness and that you will provide a caretaker whenever you are unable to look after her yourself. Impediments to keeping a cat, such as allergies or a ban on pets by your landlord, must be considered beforehand. Also keep in mind that a harmonious life together will only be possible if the cat is welcomed by every member of your family.

Mutual reciprocity: "cat people" have a special link to their pets and will quickly be accepted as "super cat."

Supplies The annual costs of keeping a cat can easily amount to $1,000 for food, litter, veterinary care, and other essentials.

Tolerance Even a well-behaved cat will occasionally scratch carpets or furniture. The cat will also shed throughout the year, especially during spring and autumn. A cat cannot be ordered around, nor can you forbid her to do certain things. Sometimes, a cat will cleverly fool her owner. Can you accept a cat's idiosyncrasies with a smile, and maybe even enjoy them?

Territory Even indoor cats without access to the outdoors need their own territory, with a special place to sleep, an eating area, and a litter box. Cats need space to roam around, spots for resting and withdrawing, and plenty of climbing and scratching opportunities. Do you have sufficient space, and are you willing to set up your home to suit a cat?

Attention Cats like to have their owners around them for at least a few hours every day for cud-

dling, petting, and playing, and as security. They want to feel, "My supercat is there for me." Giving your cat sufficient attention is the only way to establish trust between you.

Consistency Cats like it when life around them proceeds in an orderly fashion. They will need some time to adjust to a move or to their owner's new partner. In other words, avoid any major changes in your life around the time you bring your new cat home.

A Kitten or a Cat?

The characteristics of a cat person must, of course, include patience. That is particularly true with kittens. It is a lot of fun to watch kittens grow up, but it will also take its toll on your nerves! During their rambunctious period, kittens can easily upset your entire home, often bringing themselves into danger with their boundless energy and curiosity. Circumspection and caution are therefore called for, as well as the time required to care for your cat. Kittens require three to five meals a day, and you should set aside up to two hours for playing together. In addition, it takes time for a kitten to learn the ground rules for living with and accepting people.

If you have all the characteristics of a typical cat person but cannot spare the time, you don't necessarily need to forgo the pleasure of a four-footed living partner. There are many adult cats that have not yet found their owners (or have lost one). Adult cats are significantly more settled than kittens, do not exhibit any wild behavior, and usually become accustomed very quickly to a new home. Provided they have been properly socialized, they are devoted, loving, and affectionate pets. If you are a cat person, adjusting to your home should be easy for such a cat.

Cat years – Human years

At 1 year of age, cat bones fully stop growing. This occurs in people at approximately 24 years of age, give or take a few years. So, a 1-year-old cat is roughly equivalent to a 24-year-old person. From that point on, cats age approximately four years for every one human year.

17

A New Family Member

A cat must not only suit you, but she must also be accepted by your entire family. It is important for you to assess your living situation before your new cat moves in.

Start with a pair Cats are not grumpy, solitary creatures. Why not start out with a pair of them? In many kitten litters, there are siblings who like to do everything together. Even some mature pairs of cats would like to remain together for the rest of their lives. In any case, for an indoor cat that is left alone during the day, having another cat in the "territory" is the best assurance against boredom. Together with their trusted human pal, these cats will adapt more quickly to their new environment— and their owner will get a double dose of cat love. Whether you decide on two males, two females,

or a mixed pair does not matter very much: Cats that have been together from the beginning will usually also get along later in life. You will need to get your cat(s) spayed or neutered no matter what, unless you wish to breed them.

Introducing a second cat Even if you already own a cat, there are many reasons to add a second cat to your home. If you already have a mature cat, it is best to add a kitten. The kitten will adapt more quickly than an older cat, and she will be more readily accepted. Only in a few cases is this not advisable:

> Your cat is already a "senior" or is in ill health. In this case, a young cat—especially a small, temperamental bundle of energy—would be too much stress for the older cat.

> Your cat has lost a long-term partner and there is still an obvious feeling of loss. She probably will not even know what to do with a kitten. In such a case, look for an older cat that gets along well with other cats. Such a social butterfly might be found in an animal shelter, or through a rescue organization.

> Your cat has been happy for years in her solitary role and you spend a lot of time with her.

Through skillful negotiations by their owner (see page 31), most cats can adjust to each other, at least to a point where they get along. This process is usually slightly easier with neutered males than it is with females. Friendships among cats are easiest when both are similar in character or they complement each other. A cuddly lap cat has less reason to be jealous if the new cat has a more playful personality and doesn't much prefer to cuddle.

Cats love to sleep and doze. However, they also need stimulation, such as interaction with another cat.

Cautious approach! It can take some time, and lots of patience, before an older cat becomes friends with a new arrival.

Dogs and cats can get along very well—provided the human owner cleverly mediates between the two.

Cats and dogs They get along far better than conventional wisdom has it, but skillful mediation is still required (see page 31). The rather different "languages" of both can easily lead to misunderstandings. A well-trained dog will usually accept a kitten. An older cat who has had bad experiences with dogs, and distributes cautionary slaps with her paws, will less readily adapt. Certain dog breeds (e.g., terriers) find it difficult to respect cats as family members.

Other pets With some patience, large rabbits and gentle cats can learn to get along with each other. However, it is not wise to leave the two alone together. Guinea pigs and other small rodents are considered prey by cats. These animals are usually uncomfortable in the presence of their "predators," even if they are still in the safety of their cages. Such small pets probably will be far more comfortable in a room where the cat cannot gain access.

Children and cats These two generally understand each other very well, provided the children have learned to be considerate and gentle with animals. Usually this is the case with children from school age onward. In order to look after a cat independently, a child needs to be at least twelve years old. Even then, the final responsibility for the cat's care must remain with an adult.

Outdoor or Indoor Cat?

There is no question: Cats love to roam about freely. However, that is possible only where there are no cars and no hunting areas close by, and the neighbors have no objection to cats. An appropriate compromise is a fenced-in yard or an outdoor pen secured with netting (see page 53). Even a high-rise apartment can be turned into a stimulating cat territory (see pages 24–25). In such a case, it's best to choose a kitten that has been kept indoors during her principal development period (up to the seventh week after birth). She will never even miss the outdoor freedom.

Your Feline Companion

Humans and cats are ideally suited for each other, but not every cat is well suited for every human. Whether cat and owner become an incredible team depends in part on the preparation of the cat's new home. Beyond that, the breed, age, and source of the feline housemate are also important.

Fostering a Good Partnership

The first thing to consider is how to acquire a cat. For some, this decision is made by the cat, who is— for whatever reason—seeking a new family. Suddenly and quite unexpectedly she will be at your doorstep and indicate in no uncertain terms "I want to live with you." Such cats seem to have an instinctive eye for cat people, and an "adoption" usually leads to a happy relationship for the cat's entire life. However, if a cat suddenly appears on your doorstep, first check with the local animal shelters to see if anyone has reported a lost cat. Also be sure to post flyers around the neighborhood with pictures of the cat and your contact information. You want to make sure that the cat is not someone's beloved pet that went missing. If no one claims the cat after about six months, you can assume she is yours for life.

In addition, cats sometimes survive their owners or an owner (for whatever reason) suddenly can no longer provide for her cat. Maybe you know the cat already and you like her. In this case, a second-hand cat can become a first-class cat. You will know her habits and preferences, and she has already been well trained. The only thing she will need is your compassion in order to get over the upheaval in her life.

Kitten Kaboodle

There is a particular charm in watching a kitten (or two) grow up in your home. Kittens are nearly always available somewhere, and each kitten is marvelous. However, not every delightful kitten is the right partner for a particular person or a particular home. Personality development begins in the nursery: trusting and open, or more skeptical and shy? A one-owner cat or a family cat? An indoor cat or a free-roaming cat? Pay close attention to the type of environment and background in which the kitten is raised.

Decisions, Decisions . . .

Are you looking for a kitten who will gain confidence in you quickly and who has had sound "basic training"? In that case, it's vital to assess the home of your future feline companion! See where the mother cat and her progeny are living. Check that sleeping, feeding, and cat toilet areas are clean, and that the cats convey a healthy, cared-for impression. Pay particular attention to whether they are lovingly cared for by their owner and are well integrated into family life. Kittens that have grown up under such circumstances will have had positive experiences during their developmental phases (see page 13). They will quickly feel at home with you. Before you take your new cat home, be sure to confirm that she has been immunized and seen by a veterinarian. Likewise, it is important that you take your new kitten to the veterinarian for an exam a few days after bringing her

home to make sure she is healthy. Be sure to set up this appointment before you bring her home.

Pedigree Kittens

The same rules also apply to the purchase of pedigree kittens. In addition, you should get your kitten only from an established breeder! Breeder associations (see page 62) will provide you with the names of qualified breeders in your area. You can trust a breeder if he or she

> handles cats lovingly. Even a separately accommodated stud male should be part of the family and given due affection;

> does not sell kittens before the twelfth week after their birth;

> provides a purchase contract and appropriate papers (pedigree documentation, veterinary health and immunization certificates) as a matter of course;

> wants to know how the kitten is going to be looked after by you, has a lot of time for your questions, and is willing to assist you with advice after purchase.

The going rate for a pedigree kitten is at least $800. Breeding cats is a time-consuming and costly venture. Quality food is expensive, as are health care and breeders' association dues, stud fees (about $700), and setting up suitable living quarters for the cats. Participation in shows is also costly but unavoidable for breeders: Only highly rated cats are admitted to a stud program. And what do you get for your money? A healthy, friendly kitten, typical in appearance and character for her breed. She will become a lovable companion for many years, which is priceless.

A good home makes for an excellent start in life. When the mother cat trusts humans, it carries over to her little ones.

A Second Chance: Shelter Cats

Would you like to do something for animal rescue? Through animal shelters or cat rescue groups, you can find cats and kittens that have been neglected, surrendered, or simply released onto the streets. Some animal shelters are under veterinary supervision, and cat rescue organizations work together with veterinarians. Therefore, you don't need to be afraid that you are bringing a sick cat into your home; however, to be on the safe side, you must have your cat examined by a veterinarian as soon as you bring her home. Obtain as much information about the cat of your choice from her caretaker. You should also accept the fact that it may take a little longer for her to gain sufficient trust in you, or even that she may never become an easy-going family cat or one that likes to be cuddled. Nevertheless, if you give her a chance and show a lot of patience, you will gain her friendship in the end. Whether you decide on a youngster or an adult is ultimately irrelevant. Even older cats will eventually become attached to a new owner if he or she can win the cat's trust.

Adopting a Stray

Has an ownerless cat stolen your heart? This can lead to a close friendship (see page 21). However, you will need as much patience and understanding for a stray cat as for a shelter cat. You will also need a good veterinarian to examine the cat as soon as possible, free her of any parasites, and immunize her.

Some strays are unsociable and will remain so, because they have never been properly socialized to humans. If you want to help strays—but not necessarily own one—support an animal rescue project. These organizations not only provide food and proper accommodation but also have strays spayed and neutered.

How to Recognize a **Healthy Cat**

TIPS FROM
CAT EXPERT
Brigitte Eilert-Overbeck

CURIOUS BEHAVIOR is a must. Although a kitten may be tired at times, and there are differences in temperament among cats, be wary it she is apathetic and does not react to stimuli.

CLEAR EYES, no tears, no crusty buildup. The nictitating membrane (third eyelid) remains invisible.

PINK GUMS and mucus membrane, white teeth without plaque.

CLEAN NOSE without discharge. It can be slightly moist and cool or warm and dry, but it must not have skin cracks. The external ears must be clean and odorless.

SMOOTH, DENSE COAT without knots and matted patches.

TAUT, FIRM BODY with slender, but not caved-in, flanks.

CLEAN ANAL REGION without matted, dirty fur.

FAVORABLE OVERALL IMPRESSION: calm, even respiration, lithe gait, paws with smooth pads and no injuries or cracks.

Everything a Cat Needs: Essential Equipment

Once your new companion feels totally at home with you, she will consider your home and everything in it her territory and personal property. However, she will still need a few things all her own. You should buy these items before the cat moves in—she will consider it a housewarming present.

"I Scratch, Therefore I Am . . ."

. . . Lord of the manor." A large, solid scratching post and climbing tree, or an equally suitable object for sharpening claws, is essential basic equipment. Sharpening their claws is both exercise and weapon maintenance for cats, a way of indicating "I am in charge." For indoor cats you should provide a few scratching posts distributed throughout the house. Otherwise, the furniture will quickly show claw marks.

Eating and Sleeping

Cats need their own tableware. Each cat should have two dishes, one for wet food and one for dry food. The dishes should preferably be made of ceramic or stainless steel and placed on top of a washable, non-skid mat. Your cat will also need a water dish. The water dish must be kept at least 6 feet (2 meters) away from the food bowls. After eating, the cat will move to the "watering hole," just as her ancestors once did.

For napping, your cat will need a basket with a soft pillow or blanket. It may be that your new housemate will prefer to find her own sleeping site. In this case, keep a few extra blankets and pillows on hand, because cats like their beds soft!

Cleanliness and Coat Care

It's best to provide two litter boxes. If you have two cats, you will need to provide more. Place the litter boxes in a quiet but easily accessible location, far away from eating and sleeping areas. Kittens prefer a litter box with low sides. (The sides should be no more than 4 inches [10 centimeters] high; later on, the edge of the container can be higher.) Initially, you should supply the same litter that the cat is familiar with from her previous home. This will make it easier for her to adjust to her new home. Although cats largely take care of their own appearance, certain grooming tools, such as a comb and brush (see pages 37–38), should be on hand, even for shorthaired cats. For longhaired cats, you will also need a mat splitter to untangle matted hair patches. Finally, you should have a few toys—some balls, cloth mice, and bags of catnip—on hand. You are now ready to bring home your new housemate.

"Watering Holes"

LOCATION A cat will drink more when her water bowl is not placed right next to the food bowl. Drinking is particularly important when your cat's diet consists principally of dry food.
SEVERAL DRINKING SITES Distribute the water bowls around the house—for example, on various windowsills. Right next to them, place a bowl with cat grass (oat or wheat grass), and the perfect indoor oasis is ready for your pet.

WELL BEDDED Whether it is a wicker basket or a snuggle sack, cats like to withdraw to a protected place to sleep. Some cats will ignore their baskets, preferring to sleep on top of a cupboard or—if permitted—on your bed. During the day, cats often enjoy sitting where there are things to see before going back to nap. Your cat will appreciate a blanket or pillow for cuddling at these sites.

FITNESS CENTER A large scratching post is mandatory for cats. If the post has branches to allow for climbing, it is the ideal fitness center for your cat. This tree can be made even more interesting by suspending different toys from its branches: sometimes a soft-cloth mouse, sometimes a ball with an internal noisemaker. Alternatively, hang a few corks on elastic bands.

HER OWN DISH Cats must eat from their own bowls, not from plates or dishes used by humans! Select ceramic and stainless steel bowls, because plastic will develop cracks and become unhygienic.

A Warm Welcome: Helping Your Cat Adjust

When your new housemate is moving in, take your time. Set aside at least one weekend, or better still several days, so that your kitty can slowly adjust to you and process all of her new surroundings. If you are picking up your cat yourself by car, you will need a stable, waterproof, and easy-to-clean pet carrier. You will use this later for trips to the veterinarian. In addition to carriers made of hard plastic, there are also soft-sided bags that serve the same purpose. They are attractive and practical, but they are slightly on the expensive side: One of these may set you back $100–$120.

If possible, take another person along with you to pick up your cat. One of you will be able to concentrate on driving, while the other talks calmingly to the cat. Be sure to take along an item from the cat's old home, such as a blanket, pillow, or toy. Having a familiar item around will have a calming effect on the cat.

To get off to a good start, you should arrange everything so that the cat can quickly take possession of her new territory. The food dishes should already be laid out in the kitchen, the litter boxes should be positioned in protected nooks, and her sleeping basket should be placed in a draft-free corner. If you are not averse to letting the cat on your bed, then your bedroom is a suitable place to set up her bed. The scratching and climbing tree should ideally be situated somewhere between the sleeping and the feeding areas (e.g., in the hallway), angled in such a way that its various resting platforms provide excellent outlooks. This caters to two distinct feline preferences: After sleeping and before eating, cats like to demonstrate their territorial claim by using their claws, and they also love lookouts. Cave-like hiding places are favorites as well, so you should offer several such cozy dens throughout your home.

Sit on the carpet and wait patiently:
Eventually the cat will become curious
and approach you cautiously.

No cat can resist when her human companion lies on the floor and invites her to play or offers a tasty tidbit.

Caution—Household Dangers!

SAFETY CHECK This is a must before your new cat moves in! Close off all possibly dangerous hiding places. Keep household appliances that have doors (like the washing machine and dryer) and all containers with lids, tightly closed. Use bitter apple spray on all electric cables to prevent the cat from chewing on them. Place toxic plants out of reach of your cat (see page 40).

UNDER LOCK AND KEY Medications, cleaning agents, and chemicals must be locked up. Similarly, you should put away needles, yarn, rubber bands, aluminum foil, and pieces of spun wool (these are dangerous for the stomach and digestive tract), buttons and marbles, and anything else that can be swallowed. Plastic bags also present a danger; the cat could suffocate if she gets stuck inside one.

Leisurely discovery Once the new family member has arrived, close all windows and doors leading outside before opening the carrier. Position the carrier so that the litter box is directly in sight of the cat, providing an opportunity that is often gratefully accepted. After that, let the cat discover her new home. Keep an eye on her, but disturb her as little as possible and ask the other family members to show similar consideration.

A secure retreat If there are many activities going on in your home or there are other pets, it is advisable to set up a separate reception room. From there, the cat can explore the remaining rooms of the home at her leisure. Equip the reception room with a basket, feeding place, water bowl, and litter box. Of course, you will also need to provide a scratching post, but starting with an inexpensive corrugated cardboard scratcher will be fine.

Introducing Yourself

New beginnings are difficult, whether for a little kitten who has been separated from her mother and siblings, or for an older cat that suddenly finds herself in unfamiliar surroundings. You, as the "super cat," can help your cat get over this difficult period. The best way to do this is by seemingly ignoring her. You simply need to be around and talk to her in a friendly manner. Quickly interrupt any direct eye contact by blinking or briefly looking away. Cats do the same thing among themselves to indicate peaceful intentions. You can roll a little ball or dangle a piece of string, but always remain sitting on the carpet, so that both of you meet at eye level. Gently stroke the cat, but only after she has sniffed your hand. This will establish the first contact and mark the beginning of your relationship.

The Indoor Cat and Her Territory

Should your new housemate's territory lie exclusively inside your home? That eliminates many of your worries, because an indoor cat is exposed to far fewer dangers than cats that are permitted to roam freely outside. However, it also presents a challenge. After all, the cat should feel comfortable within the four walls you both share, be allowed to follow her innate preferences, and find sufficient stimuli for her natural intelligence. It is up to you to banish the biggest enemy of the indoor cat: boredom. The better you succeed in doing this, the better your living arrangement with your new housemate will be. If you decide to adopt two cats right from the start, it will be of considerable help. In addition to boredom, there is one other factor you will need to take into consideration.

All mine! The right home setup can turn an indoor feline into a proud territory owner.

Everywhere is cat territory. Indoor cats want access to the entire house or apartment. If they are to stay out of certain rooms—for example, the bedroom—then the door must be kept closed. Such territorial boundaries will generally be accepted. However, in a home suitable for cats there should only be a few such restrictions. You should provide many hiding places in nooks and behind curtains. An empty cardboard box with an entrance hole makes a mobile hiding place ideally suited for occasional surprises. If you also place several scratching posts (like sisal-covered scratchboards) at different locations, you are not only doing your cat a favor but also your furniture and carpets. Keep in mind that cats do not want to stay only on one level. Open up a second floor! With a pillow on the windowsill, a nest bed near the heater, a sisal mat in the bookcase or cupboard, or a folded blanket on top of the wardrobe, you can create attractive areas for your feline pal. You can provide climbing aids, such as a ladder or a rope, for the little adventurer. You might also consider turning a secured balcony into an open-air cat resort, which will make your cat immensely happy. If you want to secure your balcony with safety netting (available at pet shops) to convert it into a veranda, you may first need to clear the project with your landlord. Such a porch can be readily outfitted with a climbing tree, cozy cave, and a "jungle" of harmless plants, such as bamboo, green lilies, Cyprus grass, thyme, and catnip, turning it into a real cat paradise.

Dream home: Transport yourself for a moment into the dreamworld of felines. Cats like to roam through their territory and look at it from different

Sporting challenge: Thick ropes are an invitation for stretching and grasping exercises, and even for scratching, climbing, and balancing. Such ropes and a scratching and climbing tree turn even the smallest indoor territory into a real fitness center.

perspectives—preferably from above. They like to withdraw into secure hiding places, to sleep and doze, and to lay in wait for prey. They enjoy company, if and when they feel like it. You can fulfill most of these wishes for your pet. And for those wishes that you can't grant—waiting for prey and hunting— you have an excellent substitute: regular playtimes! But first, you have to eliminate all dangers.

Safety first. Dangers lurk inside as well as out. Even apparently harmless household items can be dangerous for cats (see page 27). To prevent small

cats from injuring themselves in the opening of bottom-hinged windows, install safeguards that can be purchased from home improvement or hardware stores. Inserts made of wire-mesh, fiber-glass, or nylon threads can make open windows crash-proof. Similarly, a balcony must be secured with safety netting. Caution, too, around the stove! This is one place that must be off-limits for your feline pal. After cooking, place a pot of cold water on top of hot stove burners or cooking elements so that your cat can't burn herself on them.

29

Etiquette for Cats

Cats have their own rules of etiquette. By following them, they avoid a lot of stress and misunderstanding among themselves. Your new cat will become confident more quickly and feel better understood if you also observe these rules.

What to do

(+) Say hello when you cross each other's paths. Friendly cats greet each other with a purring sound. From you, the cat will also accept a "hi there," a purr, or her name.

(+) Before stroking your cat, hold out your hand so she can sniff it. Scent checking is part of cat etiquette.

(+) Turn feeding and daily play sessions into rituals, which should always take place at the same time. Pleasant and repetitive routines convey reliability and security.

(+) Blink your eyes when you look at your cat. Among cats this represents smiling and the assurance "I do not want to bother you."

What not to do

(−) Don't just grab your cat when you want to pick her up. Being seized from above triggers fear; she feels like "prey." Better: Talk to your cat and pick her up so that one hand reaches around her chest and the other supports her rear end.

(−) Avoid renovations and furniture rearranging, until the cat feels completely secure. Even then, proceed slowly!

(−) Avoid noise and frantic activities. This alarms your cat and signals a stressful situation.

(−) Do not disturb your cat while she is sleeping or eating.

At Home with Other Animals

When there are other animals living in your home, your ability to mediate between them and your cat may be essential, along with patience and nerves of steel! The less you force the issue, the better it will work out in the end.

Cat and cat Take the new arrival to the reception room (see page 27) and pet and praise your resident cat as much as possible. Then let the new cat explore her new home while you stay in the reception room with the resident cat. Give the resident cat a few tidbits in order to establish a positive link with the odor of the newly arrived cat. Prior to the first meeting of the two cats, rub both of them with an unwashed T-shirt of yours or another article of clothing that has your scent on it. The presence of your scent will say, "We belong to the same clan," and will create a more amiable atmosphere. Praise the resident cat if she remains peaceful. After that, let both of the cats eat from food bowls placed near each other. If this works on the first try, great. But don't get discouraged if you have to repeat this ritual several times.

Cat and dog Here, too, a separate reception room has proven to be effective. The dog should be on a leash for the first encounter and the cat must be able to withdraw quickly. Concentrate on the dog and reward him with treats and praise when he ignores the cat. As soon as they seem to be tolerat-ing each other reasonably well, feed both of them in the same room but at different locations. Never permit the dog to rush at the cat, but praise and reward the dog when he approaches the new arrival gently.

Cat and small animals The cat's territory must end where the domain of small rodents, dwarf rabbits, and birds begins—at least if you want your smaller animals to live stress-free. Only cats and large rabbits can be taught to get along with each other to some extent (see page 18–19). Still, it is best never to leave the two alone together!

Rabbit whisperer: A cozy relationship can develop between "velvet-paws" and "long-ears." Nevertheless, the human owner should keep a close eye on them during their encounters.

Health and Happiness

Studies have proven it: Cat owners are more emotionally balanced and healthier than people who do not own a cat. Cats are good for your well-being! In turn, you can do a lot to help your cat lead a long, healthy, and happy life.

Keeping Your Cat in Top Form

Cats convey a lot to other cats and to us. However, they "say" little or nothing about illnesses. This taboo has been passed down from the cat's wild ancestors: Never show any weakness that might encourage possible predators! The idea of asking another cat for help is also unheard of among cats. Consequently, you need to be even more attuned to your cat's health. Fortunately, there is much you can do to ensure that your cat remains in top condition and continues to enjoy her life well into her senior years.

First-off, it is very important to feed your cat a balanced diet (see pages 34–36). This provides her with energy and supplies her body with the nutrients it needs to build lean muscle, strong bones, healthy skin, and an effective immune system. A healthy diet also encourages proper digestion. It does not require a major effort to fill your cat's dish with high-quality, nourishing food.

Prevention Is Best

Cats are clean by nature and will easily spend three hours per day grooming themselves. You should support this with proper coat care and maintenance (see pages 37–38). Regular grooming will keep many disease problems at bay. You should also monitor your cat for signs of illness (see page 23).

To ward off infections and parasites, and attend to other health problems, you will require the services of a competent veterinarian (see pages 39–40). He or she will also need to administer periodic booster immunizations (see pages 41–42). Even healthy cats need an annual health checkup. Although your cat is likely to be less than thrilled with these visits to the veterinarian, a bit of prevention is always better than a cure.

Bon Appétit! The Correct Cat Diet

Cats are meat eaters (carnivores) by nature, but they do not live on meat alone. Typical cat prey is more like a natural whole-food diet, because the little hunters also take in indigestible components such as fur, skin, and bones, as well as the stomach and intestinal content of the prey. The latter consists of pre-digested plant matter, mainly grains, and so provides essential plant supplements. In the cat's prey, protein, fat, vitamins, minerals, trace elements, and dietary fiber—all the dietary building blocks—come together in the proper proportions. Indoor cats, who hardly ever have access to prey, must be provided a properly balanced diet.

Prepared commercial foods Quality prepared foods closely approximate the "prey animal" concept, and are recommended as the basis of the feline diet. These foods address the special requirements of cats, providing high levels of certain amino and fatty acids; they contain all the essential nutrients and vital ingredients in proper amounts. This is true of both moist and dry foods. Which should you feed your cat?

Canned or dry? Dry food has its advantages. It does not spoil in the bowl, is easy to handle, and certain brands can help reduce dental plaque. Yet, as a sole food source, it must be used with caution. Moist food contains up to 80 percent water, but highly concentrated pellets of cat kibble have only 15 percent at the most. If fed only dry kibble, your cat needs to make up the moisture deficit by drinking plenty of water so that she does not sustain kidney or bladder problems. For one bowl of dry food, your cat should drink three full bowls of water. However, cats usually drink less. Therefore, it's best to give at least two thirds of the daily diet in the form of wet food and, at the most, one third as dry food. It is also important to distribute several water bowls throughout your home. Water is the

Highlight of the day for compulsive nibblers: a tasty meal. For that, some cats will literally stand on their hind legs.

Whatever prey a cat can catch during occasional hunting expeditions is—under today's territory situations—barely more than a snack between regular meals.

Caution—This Is Fattening!

KITTEN FOOD is ideal for kittens, but contains far too many calories for adult cats. From the eighth month onward, switch your feline housemate over to food appropriate for adult cats.

CAT TREATS consist mainly of grains, and should be fed only sparingly! The carbohydrates in most treats are not metabolized into energy but into fat deposits. So cats get fat but remain hungry.

HUMAN FOOD is tempting for cats. An occasional piece of meat, a sliver of liverwurst, or something similar may be appropriate, but cake, cookies, and sweets should definitely not be fed to your cat. Just two sugar cubes can cause a weight increase of 18 ounces (5 grams).

best drink for cats! Cats often cannot tolerate the lactose in milk, which is also too rich in nutrients.

How to recognize high-quality food. What a selection of cat food on the supermarket shelves! Food especially for kittens, for adults and older cats, for active cats, and cats that are lazy. All brands promise to be healthy and tasty. Yet, you can only recognize quality cat food if you read the nutrition label on the back of the package:

› Balanced cat food is designated as "Complete Diet." A product labeled as a "Supplementary Food" does not cover all nutritional requirements.

› The components are listed in the ingredients column according to their percentage in the total amount. Whatever is listed first makes up the largest portion of the food. If the first component is meat and its percentage is very high, this is indicative of quality food. The other ingredients must also be listed individually and should not be hidden under terms like "animal by-products" or, worse, "animal and plant by-products."

› In dry food, pay attention to the type of meat and how it is listed. If it is listed first with a high percentage figure, this refers only to the weight before drying—the meat component in the dry food itself is actually much smaller. If, instead of "chicken" or "chicken meat," you read "chicken meat meal" or "dried or dehydrated chicken," you can trust the percentage figure. That, too, should be as high as possible.

› Plant material (such as grains) must be included in balanced cat food, but it should not make up more than 10 percent of moist foods. For technical reasons this percentage is higher in dry foods. However, dry food with a predominant grain component is not suitable for the daily diet because a cat's metabolism cannot properly utilize it.

Plants within reach of your cat must be absolutely safe. Bamboo and Cyprus grass are good choices.

› Instead of with chemical preservatives, quality food is preserved using natural anti-oxidants such as vitamins C and E. Dyes and artificial flavors should not be ingredients in cat food, nor should sugar and caramel, which can damage teeth.

› The dietary recommendations usually refer to adult cats with a weight of 6.5 to 9 pounds (3–4 kilograms). For moist food, serve 5 to 14 ounces (150–400 grams), spread out over two meals. For dry food, 1.5 to 3 ounces (40–80 grams) should be freely accessible to your cat. Rule of thumb: The lower the recommended serving size, the more nutritious the food is.

Home Cooking

You can also prepare your own cat food. The best ingredients to use are muscle meat (beef and mutton), heart, poultry, and fish. Everything should be cooked or steamed and served without bones.

Simmer a small portion of oats, rice, barley, or noodles together with a very small amount of vegetables to make a well-balanced meal. Avoid cabbage, leeks, onions, and legumes. These tend to cause flatulence; moreover, onions can lead to anemia. Homemade cat food should only be salted very lightly—one fifth to one third the amount commonly used in human food is sufficient. If you feed your cat primarily with food you have prepared, she will need supplementary vitamins and minerals. You should discuss this with your veterinarian. It is better not to experiment: Nutritional deficiencies and excesses can both endanger the health of your cat.

Raw or cooked? Cats do not cook the mice they catch, which is one reason why they become infested with worms and other parasites. Even commercial red meat can contain pathogens, and pork can infect dogs and cats with the fatal Aujeszky virus. By cooking your homemade cat food, you definitely reduce this risk. Recently there has been much talk about the biologically appropriate raw food (BARF) diet. This diet contains quality raw meat, as well as uncooked bones and a number of supplements. Many cats seem to do well on this type of diet. However, it involves thorough training, meticulous care, and a certain amount of time and money. More information is readily available on the Internet.

Special Treats. Occasionally you can offer a pinch of butter to your feline pal, a hard-boiled egg yolk crumbled over her regular food (valuable fats and vitamins!), or a portion of yogurt or cottage cheese, which are all good for her intestinal flora.

Grooming and Hygiene

A meticulously groomed fur coat protects against the weather, repels dirt, and makes it difficult for parasites to invade your cat. Therefore, it's not surprising that cats spend more than three hours a day grooming. Give your cat a hand with this activity! While grooming her, you can keep an eye on her general health and condition, and you will notice if something is not as it should be. If your cat is used to this regimen from the start, she will enjoy the special attention. Even if your feline pal is not thrilled about your involvement, try to make grooming enjoyable for her. With some gentle coaching, praise, and a tasty treat when the whole process is over, most cats can be persuaded.

Grooming Shorthaired cats should be combed from head to tail once or twice a week, and preferably more often during the spring and fall when they shed their coats. For cats with very short fur, like Siamese and Burmese, it is often sufficient to wipe them down with a damp chamois cloth. Many cats that are not thrilled with being brushed often enjoy being massaged with a grooming glove (available at pet supply stores). Brushing off the loose hairs that your cat has not already removed will reduce the amount of fur she ingests, resulting in fewer furballs in her stomach. Longhaired and semi-longhaired cats should be brushed daily; otherwise their fur will quickly become matted. Even with frequent grooming, there will be the occasional matted knot. Remove these cautiously with a comb, and in very persistent cases with a mat splitter.

Tick control Especially during the spring and fall, outdoor cats need to be examined daily for ticks. Do this by sliding your hands over all parts of her body. Ticks are spiderlike animals that carry dangerous infections, and it is advisable to remove these parasites before they become firmly attached to your cat. Ticks that have become gorged with blood should be removed as quickly as possible with a pair of tick forceps. As a precautionary measure, you should have your cat examined by her veterinarian if she has been bitten by a tick.

Eyes and ears Crusty buildup in the corners of the eyes can be wiped away with a damp cloth or moistened cotton ball. The external ear should be cleaned in a similar manner. Some cats are inclined to develop waxy buildup in the ears. Do not use cotton swabs to clean your cat's ears, as this can result in internal ear injuries. Ask your veterinarian about the appropriate treatment method for removing the buildup and avoiding ear infections. An unpleasant

Wash my fur . . . Cats that get along well with each other sometimes even help groom each other.

37

1 EARS Your cat's ears must be clean. Traces of dirt on the cloth can indicate a mite infestation. This is a case for your veterinarian!

2 EYES Older cats are often plagued by crusty buildup in the corner of their eyes. This can be easily removed with a damp cloth or moistened cotton ball.

3 FUR Gently brush out loose hairs from the fur. This way they can't end up in the cat's stomach to form furballs.

odor, frequent head shaking, and keeping the head tilted are indications of ear mites. In this case, immediate veterinary attention is required!

Claws Cats look after their claws themselves through energetic sharpening on a scratching post and by removing claw sheaths with their teeth. Clipping the claws becomes necessary only when they are not worn down or they get caught on something. Ideally, you should have this done at a veterinary clinic.

Teeth Examine the inside of your cat's mouth regularly. A brown film or an unpleasant smell indicates the presence of dental plaque, which must be removed by a veterinarian. Prevention: Brush your cat's teeth with a toothbrush and feline toothpaste. Also useful are high-quality dry food, cooked pieces of meat that can be chewed, and special dental-care snacks.

A Well-Kept Environment

Your cat needs a well-kept, hygienic environment in order to feel comfortable. Parasites and pathogens find it difficult to survive in such an environment!

Cleanliness at the cat's dinner table Remove spilled food and wipe down the eating area daily with a wet cloth. Clean food bowls before each feeding and rinse them under hot water. Dry-food bowls should be rinsed under hot water and dried, even though the food is left out for "self-service."

Litter box hygiene Fill the litter box daily to a depth of about 2 inches (5 centimeters). Wet material must be removed daily. This is easiest to do with clumping litter. Remove the feces with a small shovel, immediately or soon after it has been deposited. The litter box should be washed in hot water and scrubbed using a mild detergent at least once a week. If your cat is infested with worms, the litter box must be treated with a disinfectant.

Fighting parasites Veterinarians carry a number of very effective treatments. If you have a flea infestation, sleeping and resting areas and curtains should be sprayed with a general flea spray up to a height of 3 feet (1 meter) above the floor. Pour flea powder into the vacuum cleaner bag, and vacuum the floor, carpets, and upholstered furniture frequently in order to eliminate these pests and their progeny.

Prevention and Treatment

Although your cat may not be thrilled with visiting the veterinarian, regular examinations are absolutely necessary for her well-being. On a visit to the veterinary office, there are many smells that are unfamiliar to your cat, other animals in the waiting room, and the scary sterile treatment table! These visits may not be popular with your cat, but they are unavoidable when it comes time for immunizations (see page 42), when she needs to be spayed (see page 13), in the event of a worm infestation, if she shows symptoms of an illness (see page 41–42) or is injured, or if you decide to outfit her with a microchip (see page 52).

Although not common, it may be possible to locate a veterinarian in your area who makes house calls. Restrict house calls to emergencies, as your cat will become very upset if she feels she is being manhandled in her own territory. Since prevention is always better than treatment, even a seemingly healthy cat needs to be taken to the veterinarian for a general examination at least once a year. The veterinarian will palpate the cat's body, listen to her heart and lungs, and examine her eyes, ears, and teeth. If needed, the veterinarian can administer any preventative medications. The problem with visits to the veterinarian is that many cats vehemently object to them and will fight you virtually all the way until they are on the examination table. Even after arriving at the clinic, some cats will act like wild tigers. Therefore, it is of paramount importance that you remain calm, and that you find a veterinarian who is familiar with such difficult patients and has a lot of patience with them.

Your Cat's Veterinarian

In order to spare your cat long rides in the car, it is best to look for a veterinarian in your area. However, more important than geographic proximity is the veterinarian's competence. Tips for finding a veterinarian can come from other cat fanciers, from animal protection associations, from breeders, and from the Internet. Yet, in the final analysis, your impression is the deciding factor in whether you have found the right veterinarian for your cat. You'll probably determine this during the first office visit.

You must hold on to your cat firmly while taking her temperature. Often, this is easier when you have a helper.

Caution—Poisonous Hazards!

TIPS FROM
CAT EXPERT
Brigitte Eilert-Overbeck

Among the most common emergencies are cases of poisoning. Dangers lurk not only outside, but in your own home as well (see page 27).

TOXIC INDOOR PLANTS Among the most dangerous plants are dumb cane, adder's-tongue, Swiss cheese plants, and poinsettia. Also toxic: all arums (such as calla), aloe, cyclamen, amaryllis, avocado, azalea, philodendron, weeping fig, hellebore, crown-of-thorns, ivy, pothos, some fern and fig species, artillery plant, Jerusalem cherry, cherry laurel, oleander, primrose, violets, spurges, desert rose, and yucca.

TROUBLESOME FLOWERS Beware of daffodils, chrysanthemums, lilies, lily-of-the-valley, narcissus, dianthus, snowdrops, and tulips. Also avoid boxwood, baby's breath, Cypress spurge, and plants treated with leaf shine spray.

KITCHEN DANGERS Avocados, beans (raw), potato leaves and shoots, spinach (raw), grapes, onions, and chocolate must always be well out of your cat's reach.

The following points suggest that you have found the right veterinarian.

> The office is well organized and nobody appears to be overworked. The details of your cat are immediately recorded in the patient files.

> The veterinarian talks to your cat while she is on the examination table.

> The veterinarian remains calm and in control, even if your cat resists treatment.

> The veterinarian and his assistants rarely need to use force during the examination and subsequent treatment.

> The veterinarian takes time to explain everything to you and answers your questions in non-technical terms.

> In emergencies, the veterinarian can be reached after normal office hours.

> You find the veterinarian likeable and trustworthy.

Relax Most cats panic because the nervousness of their human owner rubs off on them. The more you worry about the visit to the veterinarian, the more your cat will worry. You can spare your cat (and ultimately yourself) a lot of stress if you remain cool and prepare for the visit in a relaxed manner.

Get her carrier ready two days before the appointment with the veterinarian. Write down your questions as well as any observations you may wish to share with the veterinarian. On the day of the visit, inconspicuously close off your cat's usual escape routes and hiding places. Pick up your cat calmly and resolutely, carry her in your arms, and then place her in the carrier. Talk to her on the way to the veterinarian and in the waiting room. Take her into the treatment room while she is still in her carrier. Once you are back at home, a treat as a reward is in order, even if your cat may initially ignore it.

A Quick Recovery, the Easy Way

If your cat is not feeling well, leave her in peace! However, do watch her closely. Many cats that do not feel like eating or drinking will accept beef broth quite eagerly. In case of diarrhea, a teaspoonful of kaolin mixed in with food often helps. Alternatively, a small portion of mashed potatoes (without milk) can also be effective. If the cat suffers from constipation, the first thing to do is remove the dry food. Let the animal lick malt paste from your finger, offer canned sardines, or mix half a teaspoon of mineral oil in with her food.

Detective work If your feline pal is still not well after a couple of days, your veterinarian will need to have a close look at her. Write down your observations and, if needed, take a fecal sample or a small amount of vomit along to the clinic. Similarly, you should consult your veterinarian in cases of unexplained behavioral changes, excessive thirst, conspicuous weight gain or loss, or marked changes in fur and skin.

Emergency! In the event of injuries, vomiting or diarrhea with traces of blood, foam, or mucus (take

Clear eyes, a curious expression, and ears in an alert upright position—this is the picture of a healthy cat. Perhaps she has just spotted some interesting prey!

Feline **First-Aid Kit**

For emergencies, you should maintain a basic first-aid kit for your cat. It should contain the following items:

EMERGENCY INFORMATION Written information, including important telephone numbers: veterinarian, veterinary emergency service, animal rescue service, fire department, poison control center.

DOCUMENTS Your cat's immunization certificate as well as any relevant documentation provided by the breeder.

BASIC INSTRUMENT SET Forceps and scissors (both with rounded tips), tick forceps, digital thermometer, petroleum jelly (to lubricate the thermometer).

WOUND DRESSING Gauze bandages, sterile bandages (cat compatible), wound dressings, absorbent cotton, adhesive bandages.

WOUND TREATMENT Wound disinfectants, healing creams, ointments. All items must be safe for use on cats.

SYRINGES Disposable syringes (without needle) for administering liquid medication; also for giving food to a weakened animal.

PARASITE TREATMENT Flea powder and de-worming agent from veterinarian (optional).

MEDICATIONS Only those prescribed by a veterinarian.

OTHER Mylar emergency blanket or travel blanket (protection against hypothermia), cold pack (for wasp and bee stings on paws), small plastic bags (for protection around bandaged paw), disposable gloves.

a sample along), constipation with a hard abdomen, respiratory distress, seizures, or if the cat is unable to urinate, consult your veterinarian immediately.

Nursing a sick cat Ask your veterinarian for detailed advice on how to look after your sick cat. If the cat has a transmittable disease, she needs to be kept in isolation from other animals. Food and water should be placed close to her, and a litter box provided. Ongoing rest, warmth, and clean bedding support healing, as does your comforting voice.

Fending Off Infectious Diseases

Nowadays there are effective vaccines (without side effects) for some of the most dangerous feline diseases.

Feline distemper (panleukopenia) and cat flu (feline rhinotracheitis) Both of these diseases are dangerous, even to indoor cats without access to other cats. Ask your veterinarian how often booster shots are required.

Feline leukemia The feline leukemia virus (FeLV) causes incurable feline leukemia. Because it is transmitted from one cat to another, immunization is required, especially for cats that have contact with other cats. Discuss booster schedules with your veterinarian.

Rabies This fatal viral disease is transmitted via the saliva of infected animals. Immunization is essential for outdoor cats, but indoor cats should also be immunized in case they escape outside. There is now a rabies vaccine, which lasts for three years. Immunization against the incurable viral diseases FIP (feline infectious peritonitis) and FIV (feline immunodeficiency virus, the feline form of AIDs) is controversial. You should assess the usefulness and associated risks with your veterinarian.

Homeopathic Medicine

Because of the required immunizations, cats have no way of avoiding the veterinarian (see pages 39–42). Some veterinarians are trained homeopaths, and others work together with non-medical practitioners and other therapists. Although their methods can rarely be proven scientifically, practitioners of alternative medicine continue to demonstrate healing successes in humans and animals. Homeopathic treatment should not replace traditional medicine, but it can be a valuable supplement for your cat, provided both the veterinarian and the therapist are very familiar with cats.

› Natural healing substances and homeopathic remedies are used for many ailments such as eczema, allergies, colds, and bronchitis, as well as for general weakness and lack of energy.

› Bach Flower Remedies, which act principally on the emotions, can relieve some ailments. They are often used on cats that appear to be "out of balance" or that have been affected mentally by trauma, fear, aggression, or exhaustion. The famous Rescue Remedy can calm even the most excited cats.

› Acupuncture is thought to revitalize the body's energy flow. Successes have been achieved in pain treatment, degenerative joint diseases, and tendon injuries, as well as with inflammation and weakness of the immune system.

The Healing Touch

Stroking feels wonderful! However, your hands can do much more for your favorite pet. You may be interested in learning one of the following touch therapies. (Further information is available in trade magazines and on the Internet.)

Acupressure/shiatsu This method is related to acupuncture, but finger pressure is used instead of needles or a laser. Its purpose is to activate the energy lines of the body through pressure points, thus releasing tension and promoting circulation.

TTouch The animal therapist Linda Tellington-Jones developed this method of touch therapy for animals, which involves gently massaging you cat with circular motions, using your fingertips. It is believed the massage has a calming effect and reduces stress, fear, and aggression.

Reiki therapy Universal healing energy is said to flow from the Reiki provider to the receiver through this method of hand placement.

Being gently stroked by loving hands feels so good—and it helps with recuperation!

Understanding Your Cat

People who understand their feline housemates will find it easier to care for them. But don't worry; as difficult as understanding cats may seem at first, it's not as impossible as you think. A peek into the feline psyche will tell us a lot about these animals.

Nurturing a Good Relationship

Humans and cats speak different languages, but this doesn't need to be an obstacle for good communication. Cats can "read" a great deal from our tone of voice and our body language. In addition, they are incredibly well attuned to our moods. We can also study how cats "talk" (see Behavior Interpreter inside the front cover). Cats communicate with sounds, body language, and behaviors (see page 46–47). In fact, these allegedly mysterious creatures openly convey their moods to everyone around them. (see page 48–49).

Little Kings

Our feline pets are born with a domineering character, which makes sense given their ties to the "king of beasts." It is understood that cats are "king" in their home territory. But don't worry; they are inclined to come to some sort of agreement with you. Even when they are long past the kitten stage, they can still be trained (see page 50–51), provided you do not demand blind obedience. Nevertheless, cats also have an innate talent to train us, and, as in any working partnership, you need to give the other partner sufficient freedom. That doesn't necessarily mean giving your cat free rein (see page 52–53), but it does mean that you need to accept your cat as a creature with her own requirements.

Nurturing the relationship also includes spending plenty of time together (see pages 54–57). When your feline companion feels that she can always rely on you (see pages 58–59), she will pay you back with lots of love.

Cat Communication

Cats "talk" to each other. They make clear statements and thus avoid misunderstandings and fighting. However, they also talk to us and expect us to understand. That's why it's important to make an effort to acquire cat language skills.

Vocalizations. Our "silent hunters" have a rather large sound repertoire:

> "Meow" comes from the cat's childhood. A kitten uses it to say to her mother, "I need something!" Your cat is trying to tell you something very similar when she meows. Adult cats rarely ever use that sound with each other.

> Cooing and delicate meowing is how peaceful cats chat with each other, as well as with us. Reply with something pleasant!

> Snarling or explosive "spitting" is a defensive threat and bluff: The intent is to persuade the potential opponent to disappear. It often works because it sounds like the hissing of a snake, and that signals "danger" to all mammals. Cat mothers also hiss at their young when they want to drive them out of a dangerous area. You can make use of this when training your cat (see pages 50–51).

> Growling or loud snarling signals the threat of an attack. Cats also growl when they bring in their prey and sometimes when they are devouring food.

> Purring feels good and summons courage. That is why some cats purr even when they are afraid or in pain. However, in most cases it means that the cat is at peace. Sometimes the cat also purrs as an appeasement: "I am not going to hurt you; please do not hurt me either!"

Body language A cat also sends clear messages with her posture.

> An extended body and stretched-out legs: "I am in my element and I feel secure."

> A crouched position: "Something is not quite right."

> Cowering with legs bent, keeping the head low: "I am warning you: If you come any closer, I will defend myself."

Would you clean me please? With a tender head-rubbing, the kitten asks her mother to lick her fur, something the mother is not going to refuse.

> Staring at another cat: "I am stronger than you! Do you want to get beat up?'
> Head extended forward: "An interesting opponent! Maybe we should sniff each other close up."
> Lowered head: "I do not want to provoke anybody and I do not want to be provoked myself."
> "Catloaf" position with paws and tail tucked under the body: "Please do not disturb!"
> Tail erected high in the air: "Nice to see you." Also: "Follow me; I would like to show you something."

What Is Your Cat Trying to Tell You When She . . .

> rolls over to one side or onto her back? She is in a playful mood and is trying to entice you.
> offers her head or head-butts you? Your cat is asking for you to groom or stroke her. Head-butting is a friendly greeting gesture.
> rubs herself around your legs or rubs her cheeks and flanks on your legs? She is marking you with an imperceptible (for humans) odor: "You belong to me!"
> kneads you with her front paws? This is the ultimate declaration of affection: "With you I am feeling like a kitten with her mother."
> raises a paw? "Stop it or I will hit you!"
> yawns extensively? Yawning is considered to be an appeasing gesture: "I am peaceful, please be peaceful to me!"
> makes her hair stand on end and arches her back? This defensive threat is aimed at an opponent the cat is afraid of. She is trying to make herself "larger."
> has raised only the hairs on her back and on her tail? Hopefully that does not apply to you—it is a threat from a self-assured cat.
> after a reprimand from you, she looks everywhere but not at you? "I do not want to provoke you any further."

How **Cats** Learn to **Recognize** Their **Names**

TIPS FROM
CAT EXPERT
Brigitte Eilert-Overbeck

Nearly every cat can learn to respond to her name. You can make the learning process somewhat more palatable to your feline friend by linking the name to something positive.

ONLY GOOD THINGS should happen to your cat when you say her name. Use it when stroking, cuddling, feeding, and playing with her. Do not say her name when you are angry, scolding, or trying to prevent the cat from doing something.

REWARD your cat when she responds to your call. During the initial training phase, offer tasty treats; later on just pet her.

TWO-SYLLABLE NAMES are best suited for cats. Monosyllabic words sound too much like an order, and multi-syllable words are usually abbreviated in everyday usage anyway. The name should also sound pleasantly soft. Attention is (nearly always) guaranteed if your "cat hello" includes a "murr" sound, as in "Moritz" or "Morley."

"IMMEDIATELY" is an unlikely response from a cat when called by her name. Keep any impatience out of your voice when calling her, so as not to disturb the positive associations with her name.

How Cats Express Their Moods

Cats use body language to convey their moods to those around them, and their facial expressions are even more telling. Few other animals show their mood as clearly in their faces. If a cat is relaxed and in a friendly mood, her face is smooth and unwrinkled. However, when she is upset or angry, her forehead is no longer smooth and sometimes her nose is wrinkled. Similarly, eyes, ears, and whiskers can be very useful mood barometers, revealing a lot about the animal's state of mind.

The eyes Your cat's eyes are not only impressive but also very expressive, and since they are

arranged frontally—just as in humans—you can communicate with each other by means of "eye language." For instance, if you are blinking slowly and pleasantly at your cat, she will blink back obviously pleased: That is the way one smiles in cat circles! A cat is not in the mood for smiling when her eyes are closed tightly, so that the light lower eyelid markings disappear in the skin fold that has been formed. (This is particularly distinctive in striped [tabby] cats.) Such grimacing is usually accompanied by aggressive snarling. Similarly, the pupils also reveal something about the mood of the cat: A cat that is scared will display dilated pupils even in bright light. If, on the other hand, there is tension in the air or the cat feels aggressive, her pupils can narrow even in low light. An emotionally well-balanced cat takes in the world calmly and seemingly undeterred, both with looks that can melt your heart and glances that seem penetratingly cool.

The ears Cat ears are precision instruments and unerring mood barometers. If the ears are tilted slightly forward, the cat feels adventurous, is attentive, and appears to be friendly. However, when there is tension, the ears are pointed straight up. Twitching ear movements have nothing to do with playfulness; in fact, they indicate anger. This develops into a concrete threat when the ears are pressed flat back against the head—an attack

Do I attack? Or is it better to flee? The body language of this Abyssinian cat suggests that she is still uncertain.

is clearly imminent. Ears folded back and pulled down toward the sides of the head signal fear; the cat is undecided between fleeing and defending herself. Ears laid down flat against the head indicate that the animal has decided: "Now I'm going to defend myself." Then the fur starts to fly!

The whiskers A cat's whiskers serve not only as an antenna system and adornment, but also as a means of expression. Your feline housemate is contented when her whiskers are only slightly spread and directed sideways. However, if they are pressed flat against her face, this is a sign of shyness. When these tactile hairs are extended forward, the cat feels adventurous—when stalking prey, for example—or is looking forward to playing with you. In addition, you should be pleased when your pet touches your face with her whiskers: It is pure affection!

The tail Who says cats are inscrutable? Their tails reveal a lot about their moods. A relaxed cat drops her tail, possibly with the very tip slightly bent upward. A tail raised up signals joy, initiative, and sympathy. High-spirited kittens bend their tails into a question mark and leap about at the same time. Wagging the tail signals excitement, possibly in eager anticipation for a tasty treat or maybe during play. Vigorous tail swishing, however, has nothing to do with joyful anticipation—it signals irritation. When this happens during play, stop immediately! The cat feels annoyed. If, at the same time, her tail thumps the ground, her claws and teeth will soon be used. Angry cats and tomcats give the starting signal for a fight by lashing their tails with whip-like motions.

1 *Something is not quite right!* With her eyes wide open, the cat is watching something that has caught her full attention.

2 *Come on, say something!* The cat "talks" to whomever is facing her and watches closely for a reaction to her request.

3 *I don't like that!* The moving ears express increasing annoyance and defensive readiness. Do not approach!

4 *Get lost!* With hissing, spitting, and screaming, the cat is trying to drive off her opponent. However, eyes and ears reveal that she is scared!

The "Arrangement": Training Your Cat

Every well-trained kitten leaves her nursery having successfully completed "basic education." She is housetrained, has learned how to behave toward other cats, treats all family members like siblings, and is ready to come to terms with others in her territory. If only everybody was that well trained!

Yet, if you include barking orders, scolding, and punishment in your concept of cat education, you will have a difficult time ahead of you. Successful cat training means making a contract based on mutual respect. That sounds difficult, but it is a lot easier on your nerves than other methods. And it's not just for young cats: Whatever the kitten has not learned, the grownup cat can still learn with your support. Here's how it works:

A dreamy compromise: The shelf is for books—but one compartment belongs to a velvet-pawed "boarder."

Offer alternatives. Set realistic training objectives for yourself and keep the requirements of your feline housemate in mind. For instance, cats need to scratch; however, you can forbid scratching on furniture. Just offer alternatives (see Page 24)! The same applies to a taboo on hunting human calves; climbing parties, racing games, and hunting toys can provide just as much fun for the typical indoor cat. You can prohibit attacks on your indoor plants, but make sure that your feline pal always has her own greens available. Offer lots of praise when she uses the available alternatives. Praise and positive reinforcement are always the best training aids.

Discipline yourself. Even if the cat accepts you as the "trainer," a lot of potential conflict can be avoided by modifying your own behavior. Does the cat play with whatever is lying around? The solution: Don't leave anything lying around, at least not what you don't want her to have. Is she begging? The solution: Don't give her anything to eat at the human table, only in her designated food bowl. Does she push small objects from the table, cupboard, or windowsill? The solution: take those items away—it usually makes things look tidier anyway. Are the flowers in the window too tempting? Make them inaccessible! An expensive, but effective, solution is to install a sliding window for your windowsill garden.

Establish off-limit areas. It is understood that your cat is the "boss" in her territory. However, she must accept that a few areas are off-limits—for example, the stove, the kitchen cupboard, or the computer keyboard. These are areas where the cat can injure herself or cause serious damage. Stop her with a firm "no" and/or clapping your hands when she starts heading that way. Alternatively, you can blow into her face, which is reminiscent of her mother's hissing (see page 46). If she keeps it up, discourage her by placing double-sided adhesive tape on those sites. Once her paws get sticky, she will avoid that particular site and you can remove the tape. However, you should limit yourself to only a few forbidden areas, and to make up for it you should create a few appealing "cat sites" (see pages 26–27) especially for her.

Limit punishment. Never get carried away with punishment or verbal abuse! Both will scare your cat. Besides she can't relate your reaction to the misdemeanor that took place such a long time ago (at least in her mind). If you catch her as she is about to do something undesirable, stop her with a firm "no" and clap your hands. Another effective method is squirting water from a water pistol, or giving her a sudden scare with an unpleasant sound, like dropping keys to the ground or shaking a can with a handful of dried beans inside. Remember: This should be done in such a way that the cat does not notice it is you causing the distraction.

Try a clicker. Do you know what a clicker is? It's a mechanical device (available from pet shops) that has been used successfully in dog training. The principle behind this device is that as soon as the animal exhibits the desired behavior there is a "click," which is immediately followed by a reward. You can use a clicker to train your cat to scratch her scratching post instead of your sofa. The initial steps are easy: Put a few tasty treats in your pocket, and watch your cat. Is she looking at the scratching post? Make a "click" and immediately give her a treat. Is she walking toward it? Again, "click" and reward. Is she digging her claws into the tree? Again, "click" and reward, and add a big dose of praise. The cat should learn that "click" means "Well done! Now here is your reward." If the "click" always occurs at the very moment the action is taking place, the cat will relate it to her action. She will then correct her behavior more and more frequently, even when the tasty treats are replaced simply by praise.

Cats who have such wonderful scratching opportunities available are rarely tempted to sharpen their claws on expensive upholstered furniture, carpets, or wallpaper.

Safely Roaming Outdoors

You live in a quiet neighborhood, have a beautiful yard, and would like to open a door to the outside for your new feline housemate. As soon as your cat feels comfortable in her home and is familiar with her surroundings, you can consider a "territory extension." This is not an easy decision because outdoor cats live a dangerous existence, even in quiet neighborhoods. Check your surroundings before you let the cat out of your home. Consider the following points of concern:

> heavy road traffic in close proximity
> dangerous dogs in the neighborhood
> hunting areas adjacent or close by
> agricultural activities close by (pesticides!)
> construction sites
> "wild" toms in the area who have not been neutered (they can transmit diseases while fighting)

You should also feel out the mood in the neighborhood. Many gardeners and bird lovers are not happy about outdoor cats in their yards. Establish communication with these people and show that you understand their concerns—this is the only way your cat will have a chance to be understood and tolerated by them.

Open run. Can you risk it? If so, ensure the safety of your cat! Specifically:

> have your cat properly marked, either microchipped or tattooed, and registered by a central database. This will increase your chances of finding your cat if she gets lost. The best method is microchipping, where a veterinarian injects a grain-sized microchip with an identification number underneath your cat's skin. This chip can be read by a scanner. You can also have your cat's ear tattooed; however, this requires an anesthetic.

> Always ring a bell at dinnertime. This will attract your cat if you can't find her.

> Although cats like to roam at night, after sunset they should be kept indoors. This avoids the dangers posed by road traffic (headlights from oncom-

"Always be alert!" ought to be the motto for outdoor cats. They are constantly on the lookout for dangers, such as a steep stream bank.

Boredom? Free-roaming cats can hardly complain about that: There is always something interesting to see.

ing cars virtually paralyze animals in the middle of the road). It prevents encounters with other nocturnal hunters, such as coyotes and cat thieves.
› Permit your cat to roam freely only after she has been spayed and received all necessary immunizations.

The Compromise: Limited Freedom

Even in a quiet residential area, it is sometimes necessary to limit your cat's outdoor access because the risks involved are too great. A secure outdoor run in your own yard can be an alternative. However, even that needs to be given thorough consideration. If you want to fence in your yard so that your cat cannot get out, you'll need a mesh fence with iron fence posts that are 7.5 feet (2.3 meters) high and angled inward at a height of 6 feet (1.8 meters). Alternately, you can decide to use a 6.5 feet (2 meters) length of cat safety netting strung between telescopic posts. Another possibility is a fenced-in outdoor enclosure with a wire-mesh ceiling that can be used as an open-air resort and adventure playground. However, before proceeding with any of the above projects, make sure that they are permitted under your local building regulations. Often, such projects need a permit or approval from your homeowners' association. It is nearly always possible to enclose your balcony or veranda using cat netting. There's no guarantee that your cat won't "escape" any of the above enclosures. Keep a close eye on your cat if you plan to let her outside, even if the area is enclosed.

Cats and the Law

HUNTING Cats are considered a protected species in the United States, and cannot be hunted by humans.
BIRD PROTECTION In some areas, free-roaming cats are prohibited during the bird breeding season. If you see juvenile birds or highly protective adult birds around, keep your cat indoors.
NEIGHBORS To some extent, neighbors must accept the fact that cats roam through their yards. If your cat causes damage to your neighbor's yard, be courteous and offer to pay for or repair any damages.
AVIAN INFLUENZA (Also known as bird flu) Viruses that occur naturally among birds. Birds worldwide carry the viruses in their intestines, but usually do not get sick from them. Domestic cats can become infected by eating infected birds, and those cats can then spread the infection to other cats through feces, urine, and secretions from the respiratory tract. For this reason, don't allow your cat near poultry.

Playtime for You and Your Pet

Cats know what is good for them: lots of beauty sleep and leisurely daydreaming, alternating periods of alert observation and just watching the world go by, rigorous coat care—and action! That's where you come in! Even for felines who play and roughhouse with other cats, playing with you is among the highlights of their day. It can be the same for you; when you play with your cat, you forget stress, annoyances, and worries. You can get out of a bad mood and quickly pick yourself back up. Go down onto the ground when you play with your cat—your feline housemate enjoys encounters at eye level. Reserve at least an hour to an hour and a half of playing time a day. This sounds like a lot, but it doesn't need to be done all at one time. Extend playtime over the entire day: five minutes here, ten minutes there, a few sessions of 15 to 20 minutes each.

The play schedule There is nothing stopping you from starting the day with a short round of games. Even though it may be difficult for you to get going in the morning, your cat will show you how to mobilize your energy. If there is an opportunity for play during the day, take advantage of it! However, a cat's principal play period starts in the early evening hours and can go well into the night. At dusk, these little hunters become particularly

Diving in! Cats can have a lot of fun in a box with rustling paper.

How can I get the ball out of there? Cats enjoy toys that present a challenge—and can be pushed around energetically!

active, and often their favorite human finally comes home from work. By then cats are generally well rested. Even cats that are able to roam around outside enjoy playtime in the evening. Just a quick game before turning in and everybody goes happily to bed—or into her basket.

What to play with? So-called cat teasers (wands with plush "prey" attached to a line) and feather dusters (rods with colorful feathers)—both available from pet shops—as well as soft cords, strings, or an old braided belt, are all useful implements at playtime. In short, anything that moves or can be moved, is about the size of a mouse, and possibly also makes noises, like rustling and crackling sounds, makes a great toy. Specifically, fur and plush mice, balls with filling that rustles (preferably with a soft cover), solid rubber balls, little sacks or socks filled with catnip, paper balls, walnuts (they roll around nicely in an irregular pattern), empty (!) yarn spools, and rubber balls can certainly keep your cat busy.

Safety first Do not leave cords and toys with strings attached lying around, as your cat can get entangled in them. Remove pinned-on eyes and noses from toy mice, as well as the foil strips from feather dusters, and examine any toys purchased for attached bells and other small bits and pieces that can be swallowed. Cat toys must not be smaller than a ping-pong ball. Beyond that, anything with sharp edges or points must be avoided.

Popular Games for the Feline Hunter

Cats are predators, and so most cat games revolve around "prey": following it and catching it or searching for it.

Ball games Sit comfortably on the floor, make a little ball "magically" appear out of your pocket, and

On an undercover mission: Cats love playing hide and seek—especially when their human owner is looking for them.

show it to your cat; then roll it on the floor. Maybe she will bring it (or kick it) back to you, and the game will start over again. Cats are very good at kicking! Anyone for a game of "cat rugby," using a walnut instead of a ball? Or how about squash? Simply throw the rubber ball against a wall and have your pet catch the returning ball. It is best not to use a firm rubber ball, which has too much bounce.

Chasing objects You can entice your feline pet to follow you throughout the house with a cat teaser, or with a cord that has a toy mouse, paper ball, or some other "prey" attached. Wiggle the wand or a cord along the carpet; also try pulling it underneath a small throw rug. Caution—cats may lead the prey into corners and under wardrobes, over chairs and couches, and up the climbing tree. From time to time, let the hunter "capture the prey" so that she does not lose interest.

55

Playing catch Let the prey at the end of a toy fishing rod dance through the air and make sure that on about every third attempt the cat actually catches the prey. Extremely fun toy fishing rods such as the "Da Bird," which imitates a flying bird with rotating feathers, are available through pet supply catalogs.

Hunting game Cut one hole into two opposite sides of a cardboard box, and place the box upside-down on the floor. Push a feather duster through the two holes. Twirl the feather duster briefly and suddenly withdraw it back into the box when the cat is trying to paw it. After about three attempts, allow her to win and pounce on the prey!

Search game Cut holes into a shoebox and place a toy or a few tasty treats inside. Will the cat be able to fish these items out of the box with her paws?

Ideal toys. Of course, there are many more possibilities for exciting cat games. Your cat can always amuse herself with a plush mouse, or little balls or bags of catnip. Pet shops offer a wide range of stimulating toys such as "Play 'N' Scratch," which entices a cat to simultaneously scratch, fish, and capture, or the "Cat-Track," a type of cat roulette, where the ball needs to be fished out of a container. Many toys can be attached to the climbing tree or simply to a door. Crackle sacks and funnels are also a lot of fun. You can buy your cat all the

Pouncing onto toys with all their physical force, cats can keep themselves occupied for quite awhile, especially with items that can be moved around.

toys in the world, but they are only fun if you, the pet owner, are at the other end of them. (That is how your cat feels about it.) Be sure to leave only a few of these toys at your pet's disposal. The rest should go into a toy chest and occasionally exchanged to prevent boredom.

Life's Little Pleasures

Somewhere along the line, something other than play becomes important, even for the most exuberant cat: cuddle time! How enjoyable for your cat to have her back, flanks, and chest gently stroked (less so the belly), and how pleasant it is when you scratch gently behind her ears, along her neck, and between her shoulder blades with your fingertips. There is only one thing for her to do: purr and enjoy! Your cuddling and purring pet is not the only one enjoying this; she also does you a lot of good at the same time. For humans, such cuddle sessions are also pure relaxation. Anyone with a purring cat on his or her lap enjoys it—not only because it is comfortable, but because vibrations from the cat's body act like a gentle massage. Your cat turns into a purring massage therapist.

We can also learn a few things from a cat's stretching. Every time your cat gets up from a nap, she stretches. Do the same thing she does: it's good for your circulation, limbers up the body, and wakes you up. Look at the many "rest" pauses she takes! You should try this yourself. When nobody is looking, seemingly collapse, and then extend your body to its full height again: You will feel refreshed and more active. And the daily rat race? Your cat is not impressed with it. She approaches things slowly, assesses the situation, and waits fully focused for the correct moment to act.

Full concentration: It wouldn't be easy to distract this playful little feline from the task at hand.

Dealing with Changes

Now and then, introduce a bit of "action" to your cat's territory, change her diet (but not too much!), present new ideas for a game, or give her something new to sniff at and take possession of—these are the changes cats like. Otherwise, they prefer that everything remain "as usual" in their home. However, sometimes change is unavoidable, and your feline pal will need to adjust to something new.

Going on Vacation

You need a change of scenery, but your cat detests it. If your familiar cat sitter cannot come, you will need to find someone else to look after your pet.

The sitter search Your veterinarian may be able to help you, or you can consult the local animal protection organization. You can find free nationwide "sitter exchanges," operated by private animal support organizations, on the Internet. Animal lovers offer sitter services, often based on reciprocity. However, the exchange operators cannot screen interested parties for their suitability. Arrange for a meeting when you have found someone in your neighborhood and get to know each other. Your cat should also be permitted to check out the prospective sitter first.

Boarding your cat Many animal boarding facilities are operated with love and expertise, but some are not. It is essential that you find out personally how the animals are accommodated, and how the operators approach hygiene and health. Is the facility taking in only immunized animals that are free of parasites, and is there veterinary supervision? Will your cat get a single room if communal accommodation does not work out? Will your cat have to eat what is put in her food bowl or will she get her customary food?

Traveling with your cat Sometimes your cat simply has to come along. Whether it is by car or by train, your pet should not have to endure more

If given the choice, cats would always prefer to remain home. However, if you need to take your cat with you somewhere, her familiar carrier is the safest mode of transport.

than eight to ten hours of traveling time. The feline passenger should travel in her familiar carrier. Four hours before embarking on your trip, stop giving your cat food; she should be given nothing to eat during the trip. Every two hours, offer her water to drink. If she is used to a harness and leash, give her some toilet rest stops during the journey. If that is not possible, line her carrier with several layers of disposable diapers, which can be changed quickly if need be. Contact federal- and state public health authorities about immunization and travel regulations if necessary. For details about air and train travel with your feline pet, contact the relevant airline or rail line.

Moving

Moving can be extremely stressful, especially for cats. Fortunately, it's not very difficult to spare your cat unnecessary excitement. Completely empty the smallest room of the entire home (or the bathroom). Then place your cat's padded carrier in that room, and maybe an additional cat bed, her water bowl, some dry food, and her litter box. Also provide a few toys or a piece of bubble wrap (a very popular toy!). Lock the cat in that room before the moving crew arrives and the chaos actually starts. Don't worry; your cat will endure the confinement easier than all of the bustle in the rest of the house. Once in your new home, again set up the smallest room with all the essentials and lock your cat in there. Do not let the cat out until at least half of the furniture is in its new place and the moving crew has left. Then she can inspect everything and recognize all the familiar smells. Provide your cat with a lot of reliable routine activities over the next few days and weeks. You should let her outside only after she feels really at home in this new place.

Saying Good-bye

TIPS FROM
CAT EXPERT
Brigitte Eilert-Overbeck

Unfortunately, not all cats will pass away peacefully in their sleep after a long life. Very often, death approaches with old-age ailments, disease, pain, and suffering. There comes a time when medicine can no longer help and you have to make the difficult decision to have your loving pet put to sleep (euthanasia).

REMEMBER: You are not deciding whether your cat should live or die, but instead whether she should continue to suffer or not. The only thing she will notice about being put to sleep is the small pinprick of the anesthetic injection. Until that moment, your pet will feel secure as you hold her on your lap, gently stroking her and talking to her.

THE GRIEF will remain, but it is easier to bear when you can talk to others about it.

YOUR CHILDREN may be experiencing the death of a beloved creature for the first time. Support them, listen to them, remember all of the adventures they shared with their little friend, and, together, let your emotions out.

A

Abyssinian, 10
Acquisition of a cat, 21–23
Acupressure, 43
Adjusting to a new home, 26–27
Adoption, 21, 23
African wildcats, 7
Age equivalence, 17
Allergies, 62
Angora cats. *see* longhaired cats
Animal shelters, 23
Asian Leopard Cats, 9
Associations, 62
Avian influenza, 53

B

Bach Flower Remedies, 43
Balance, 6, 14
BARF (biologically appropriate
    raw food), 36
Baskets, 24, 25
Bastet, 7
Beds, 24, 25
Bengal, 9
Biologically appropriate raw
    food (BARF), 36
Bird flu, 53
Birds, 53
Birman, 11
Biting, 64
Blinking, 27, 30, 48
Boarding, 58–59
Body language, 46–49
Books, 62
Boredom, 28
Breeders, 22
Breeding, 12
Breeds, 7–11
British Shorthair, 9
Burmese, 7

C

Canned food, 34–36
Cat flu, 42

Changes, 58–59
Characteristics of breeds, 8–11
Children, 19
Claws, 14, 24, 26, 38
Clickers, 51
Climbing trees, 24, 26
Coats, 14, 23, 33, 37
Communication, 13, 45–49
Confidence building, 13
Costs, 17, 22
Cuddle sessions, 57
Curiosity, 23

D

Death, 59
De-worming, 62
Diana (goddess), 7
Diarrhea, 41
Diet, 33–36
Dinner bells, 52
Diseases, 41–42, 53, 62
Dishes, 24
Dogs, 19, 31
Domestication, 7
Driscoll, Carlos, 7
Dry food, 34–36

E

Ears, 14, 37–38, 48–49
Egyptian mythology, 7
Emergency situations, 41–42
Equipment, 24–25
Estrus (heat), 12–13
Etiquette, 30. *see also*
    communication
European Shorthair, 7
Euthanasia, 59
Eyes, 14, 23, 37, 48

F

Fear, 64
Feline distemper, 42
Feline immunodeficiency virus, 42
Feline infectious peritonitis, 42

Feline leukemia, 42
Feline rhinotracheitis (cat flu), 42
Felis bengalensis, 9
Felis silvestris lybica, 7
Female cats (queens), 12
Fenced-in enclosures, 53
First-aid kits, 42
Fleas, 38
Food, 33–36
Food, toxic, 40
Food and water dishes, 24, 25, 38
Forest cats, 7
Fur, 14, 23, 33, 37–38

G

Games, 55–56
Gods, cats as, 7
Grooming, 37–38
Grooming tools, 24
Growling, 46
Guinea pigs, 19
Gums, 23

H

Hair-raising, 47
Head-butting, 47
Health benefits of owning, 33
Healthy cat checklist, 23
Hearing, 14
Heat (estrus), 12–13
Hissing, 46
History, 6–7
Homemade food, 36
Homeopathic medicine, 43
Housebreaking, 64
Human food, 35
Hunting, 6–7, 14
Hygiene, 37–38

I

Illnesses, 41–42, 53, 62
Immunizations, 22, 42, 62
Imprinting phases, 13
Indoor cats, 19, 28–29

Insurance, 62
Isis, 7

K

Kittens, 12–13, 17, 21
Kneading, 47

L

Leopardette, 9
Litter boxes, 24, 38
Longevity, 16
Longhaired cats, 7, 37

M

Maine Coon, 7, 8
Male cats (toms), 13
Meows, 46
Microchips, 52
Moving, 26–27, 59
Multiple cats, 18, 31
Mythology, 7

N

Names, 47
Neighbors, 52–53
Neutering, 13
New home, adjusting to, 26–27, 59
Norwegian Forest Cat, 7
Noses, 14, 23
Nutrition, 33–36

O

Off-limits areas, 50–51
Organizations, 62
Other pets, 19, 31
Outdoor cats, 19, 52–53

P

Panieukopenia (feline distemper), 42
Parasites, 38, 62
Paws, 14
Pedigreed cats, 22

People and cats, 16–17
Persian, 7, 8
Pet carriers, 26, 58–59
Pet sitting, 58
Plants, toxic, 40
Playing, 54–57
Poisons and poisoning, 40
Postures, 46–49
Prepared commercial foods, 34
Preventative care, 33, 39
Punishments, 51
Purring, 46

Q

Queens (female cats), 12

R

Ra, 7
Rabbits, 19, 31
Rabies, 42
Raw food, 36
Registration, 62
Reiki therapy, 43
Rescue cats, 23
Rescue Remedy, 43
Rodents, 19, 31
Roman mythology, 7
Ropes, 29
Rubbing, 47
Runaways, 64
Russian Blue, 10

S

Safety issues, 27, 29
Scratching posts, 24, 26, 50–51
Second cats, 18, 31
Semi-longhaired cats, 7–8, 11, 37
Senses, 14
Shelter cats, 23
Shiatsu, 43
Short-haired cats, 7, 9, 37
Siamese, 7
Siberian, 7, 11
Snarling, 46

Socialization, 13, 23, 30–31
Spaying, 13
Spitting, 46
Stimulation, 28
Stray cats, 21, 23
Stretching, 57

T

Tails, 14, 49
Tattooing, 52
Teeth, 38
Territory, 17, 26, 28–29, 50–51
Ticks, 37
Toms (male cats), 13
Tongues, 14
Toxic plants and foods, 40
Toys, 24, 54–57
Training, 45, 47, 50–51, 64
Traveling, 58–59
Treats, 35, 36
Touch (touch therapy), 43

U

Urine, 13

V

Vacations, 22, 58–59
Vaccinations, 22, 42, 62
Veterinarians, 39–40
Virgin Mary, 7
Vision, 14
Vocalizations, 46
Vomiting, 41, 64

W

Water and water dishes, 24, 25, 34, 38
Weaning, 12
Whiskers, 14, 49
Witches, 7

Y

Yawning, 47

Cat Associations

> American Association of Cat Enthusiasts (AACE)
P.O. Box 321
Ledyard, CT 06339
(973) 658-5198
www.aaceinc.org
> American Cat Fanciers Association (ACFA)
P.O. Box 1949
Nixa, MO 65714-1949
(417) 725-1530
www.acfacat.com
> Canadian Cat Association (CCA)
289 Rutherford Road, Suite 18
Brampton, Ontario
Canada L6W 3R9
(905) 459-1481
www.cca-afc.com

> Cat Fanciers Association (CFA)
1805 Atlantic Avenue, P.O. Box 1005
Manasquan, NJ 08736-0805
(732) 528-9797
www.cfainc.org
> Cat Fanciers Federation (CFF)
P.O. Box 661
Gratis, OH 45330
(937) 787-9009
www.cffinc.org
> The International Cat Association (TICA)
P.O. Box 2684
Harlingen, TX 78551
(956) 428-8046
www.tica.org
> National Cat Fanciers Association (NCFA)
10215 West Mount Morris Road
Flushing, MI 48433-9281
(810) 659-9517
www.nationalcatfanciers.com/info.html
> Traditional Cat Association, Inc. (TCA)
P.O. Box 178
Heisson, WA 98622-0178
www.traditionalcats.com
> United Feline Organization (UFO)
P.O. Box 3234
5603 16th Street West
Bradenton, FL 34207
(941) 753-8637
unitedfelineorganization.net

Miscellaneous Organizations and Agencies

> American Humane Association
63 Inverness Drive East
Englewood, CO 80112-5117
(303) 792-9900
www.americanhumane.org

> American Society for the Prevention of Cruelty to Animals (ASPCA)
424 East 92nd Street
New York, NY 10128-6804
(212) 876-7700
www.aspca.org

Insurance

> Contact your personal insurance company for details.

Registration

> Contact your local animal welfare organization; some areas do not require cat registration.

Books

> Arrowsmith, Claire and Francesca Riccomini. *What If My Cat . . .* Barron's Educational Series, Inc., Hauppauge, New York, 2008.
> Bessant, Claire. *The Cat Whisperer.* Barron's Educational Series, Inc., Hauppauge, New York, 2002.
> Davis, Karen Leigh. *The Cat Handbook.* Barron's Educational Series, Inc., Hauppauge, New York, 2000.
> Helgren, J. Anne. *Communicating With Your Cat.* Barron's Educational Series, Inc., Hauppauge, New York, 1999.
> Helgren, J. Anne. *Encyclopedia of Cat Breeds.* Barron's Educational Series, Inc., Hauppauge, New York, 1997.
> Ludwig, Gerd. *300 Questions About Cats.* Barron's Educational Series, Inc., Hauppauge, New York, 2007.

Important Note

> Immunizations and de-worming of your cat are essential, so as not to endanger people and fellow animals.

> At the first sign of disease or parasite infestation, consult your veterinarian immediately. This will protect both your pet and you against infectious disease.

> Anyone with cat allergies should consult a medical practitioner before getting a cat.

> General liability insurance may protect against damages caused by cats—ask your agent.

German edition by Brigitte Eilert-Overbeck

English translation by U. Erich Friese, St. Ives, NSW 2075, Australia

All inquiries should be addressed to:
Barron's Educational Series, Inc.
250 Wireless Boulevard
Hauppauge, NY 11788
www.barronseduc.com

ISBN-13: 978-0-7641-4284-0
ISBN-10: 0-7641-4284-4

Library of Congress Control No.: 2009015057

Library of Congress Cataloging-in-Publication Data
Eilert-Overbeck, Brigitte.
[Katzen. English]
Cats/ Brigitte Eilert-Overbeck. – 1st ed. for the U.S.
      p. cm. – (A complete pet owner's manual)
Includes index.
ISBN-13: 978-0-7641-4284-0
ISBN-10: 0-7641-4284-4
1. Cats. I. Title.
SF447.E37513 2009
636.8—dc22   2009015057

PRINTED IN CHINA
9 8 7 6 5 4 3 2 1

The Author

Brigitte Eilert-Overbeck has been
an enthusiastic cat hobbyist for
many years. She has studied the
behavior of these fascinating
animals intensively. She was in
charge of the "Woman and Family"
segment for the German TV series
Hearing and Seeing. She has also
written numerous articles on the
subject of pets and several books
on cats, as well as articles for cat
magazines.

The Photographer

Monika Wegler is one of the best
pet photographers in Europe.
In addition, she is a successful
journalist and animal book author.
For further information visit her web
site at *www.wegler.de.*

Photo References

All photos in this book are from
Monika Wegler, except for:
U. Juniors/Schanz: p. 11 (right);
R. Schneider: p. 50; Jürgen Römer:
photograph of the author.

SOS – What to Do?

Vomiting

PROBLEM: The cat vomits hair clumps, accompanied by unusual alarming sounds.
SOLUTION: Fresh cat grass makes vomiting easier, and should always be kept on hand. Regular brushing ensures that many of the loose hairs do not end up in the cat's stomach.

Scared Cat

PROBLEM: The cat is easily frightened and appears insecure. **SOLUTION:** Provide your cat with unobstructed and peaceful retreat opportunities, and check the surrounding area. Could it be that a rival has entered the territory through the cat door? If so, consider buying a cat door with a magnetic code that will open only for your cat with a special security collar. This keeps other, uninvited cats out.

Runaway

PROBLEM: The cat escapes but is close by.
SOLUTION: Take your cat's carrier and slowly approach the cat in a zigzag walking pattern. Do not look directly at the cat, and whisper some calming words. When you are close enough, put the basket on the ground as a "retreat cave" for your cat.

Not Housebroken

PROBLEM: The normally housebroken cat has urinated on the bed.
SOLUTION: First, off to the veterinarian! Often there is a bladder problem behind such behavior. Less often, the cat is dissatisfied with the litter box. If everything is fine with the litter box, this could be a stress problem triggered by recent changes. Maybe a new member of your household? In this case, let that person do some of the feedings and other cat "services," so that a degree of trust develops between the two of them. Make sure that there are no traces of urine left behind on the bed (as that could stimulate a repeat performance). Try replacing a fluffy bed cover with a smooth one, or periodically covering your bed with a painter's drop cloth or plastic sheet.

Biting Attack

PROBLEM: Instead of letting you pick her up for a cuddling session, the cat bites. **SOLUTION:** Wait until the cat comes onto your lap on her own. For cats, the defensive reflex takes over when they are held against their will, and they will defend themselves. Therefore, let her make the first move!